STUCK
IN THE PROCESS

Sheena Marie Williams

Copyright © 2023 by Sheena Marie Williams

All rights reserved. No part of this book may be reproduced by any mechanical, photographic or electronic process, or in the form of a phonographic recording; nor may it be stored in a retrieval system, transmitted or otherwise be copied for public or private use-other than for "fair use" as brief quatations embodied in articles or reviews-without prior written permission from the author.

The author of this book does not dispense medical advice or prescribe the use of any technique as a form of treatment for physical, emotional, or medical problems without the advice of a physician, either directly or indirectly. The intent of the author is only to offer information of a general nature to help you on your quest for emotional and spiritual well-being. In the event you use any of the information in this book for yourself, the author and the publisher assume no responsibility for your actions.

All scriptures are taken from The New Living Translation Version of The Bible 1 unless otherwise noted.

Cover Design by: Heather Clark

Headshot Photographer: Maggie Lawler

Original Art Work by: Christiana Williams

See more from this author at www.sheenamariewilliams.com

ISBN # 979-8-218-96349-1

Published by Logos Publishing, LLC 2023

Dedication

I dedicate this, my first book, to my grandmother Kattie Holder who passed away June 14, 2023, before the book's completion. Grandma — I am who I am today because God used you to show me how to love others even in the difficult times. I thank you Lord for her life; she was truly a light in darkness.

Table of Contents

Acknowledgements 9
Prelude 11
1. **Unprocessed** 15
2. **Processing** 21
    The Process of Sanctification
    (The Life Cycle of a Butterfly) 31
3. **Process 1: Put God First** 33
4. **Process 2: Let God Lead** 37
5. **Process 3: Don't Get Distracted** 41
    Phase 1- Our Yes/The Egg 45
6. **Process 4: Press In** 47
7. **Process 5: Walk by Faith Not by Sight** 51
8. **Process 6: Heart Posture** 55
    Phase 2- Servitude/Caterpillar 60
9. **Process 7: Continue to Choose His Way** 61
10. **Process 8: Know His Voice** 67
11. **Process 9: Trust His Word** 71
    Phase 3- Consecration/Chrysalis 74
12. **Process 10: His Promise** 75
    My Prayer For You 79
    Phase 4- Disciple/The Butterfly 80
13. **Embracing the Process** 81
End Notes 84

Acknowledgements

First, thank you, Jesus, for leading me to this moment. I would like to thank my community for helping me with this book. Each one of my loved ones has been a pillar supporting me becoming the woman that God has created me to be and walking in what He has called me to do. To each spiritual leader, mentor, sister and brother in the faith: You all mean the world to me! I won't call you all by name, but you know who you are. Thank you for your support.

I would like to thank my mother, Kathleen, for leading me to Jesus. As a first-generation Christian living for Christ out loud, you did all that you knew was best and I would not be who I am if it weren't for the seeds planted by you. I would like to thank my spiritual father and mother, Philip and Tracie, for loving me as your own. You two have shown me what it means to be family in Christ. Thank you to my mentor, Karen. Your wisdom has taught me so much when it comes to being a woman of God. To my pastor, Ebenezer, thank you for being relentless in teaching the word of God in a way that makes it applicable. Under your leadership God has worked in me more than any other.

Last and never least, I must give a special thank you to my husband, Chris, for being the vessel that God would use to show me His undying love for us. You have no idea what you and our children mean to me. You, Lil Chris, Daniel, Christiana, Sierra, and Michael are why I want to become the best version of myself. You have lovingly lived with the broken version of me, and it seems only fitting that the healed version of me expresses gratitude to you until my last breath while telling the world of the goodness of our Heavenly Father.

Prelude

Could you imagine being grown, married for 18 years with children that range from eight-18 years of age and finding out that you have the emotional age of a 13-year-old? Well, that is my story, which is what I am going to share with you in this book. I will speak of a time in my life where God took me through a journey of expedited emotional growth. I was at a place in my life where I accepted that my 18-year marriage was going to end and my excuses for leaving would have all revolved around my husband. I was so blind to myself that I could not see the parts that I played that were self-destructive. Had I left my marriage, I would have taken the same brokenness into the next relationship. This moment in my life was when I realized that I was stuck in the process. It was time for me to face the inner little girl that had dictated many of my decisions. It was time for me to allow the unprocessed emotions that existed well before my husband's time, to heal.

I truly believe that this process happened for me rather miraculously because in this chapter of my life I was seeking God like I never had. I was sick of myself and the cycles in which I inwardly struggled. Then, my breakthrough came literally in 1,000 pieces. God used a puzzle. Yes! You read that correctly; He used a puzzle to change my life. He knows how to reach us all in special ways. So as the Word of God says, "Come close to God, and God will come close to you. Wash your hands, you sinners; purify your hearts, for your loyalty is divided between God and the world." (James 4:8) God heard my cries and it was God and God alone that is the reason that I am still happily married today, and the inner little girl has now become healed and whole. I invite you to set out on this journey with an open heart and a made-up mind that the word of God is the foundation for all *your decisions. When I was led to write this book, I was also led to ask that you fast while reading this book. Ask God what that would look like for you per your individual situation. I will only state that a biblical fast is one in which you consume water only for a stated number of days. I know that some fasts call for consuming water only for a stated amount of time in a day. Again, I say that this will vary for each of you. Be led by the Holy Spirit. I would also like to give a trigger warning because I will discuss topics of molestation and sexual assault. Before you read any further please say this prayer...*

Take a Minute to Pray and Process

*Heavenly Father, please reveal to me how you will have me to prepare for this reading. Help me to be open to your Word and what it is that you have in store for me in this book. Lord, let me be a sponge, willing to learn new things while you reveal to me the old things that I must unlearn. Give me your strength to look back on my past and to let the things go that have kept me stuck. Let this moment in my life be a moment that I choose your will above my own. I know that you can change my circumstances with **(insert a specific prayer point here)**_____. I trust you Lord and I ask that you have your way in my life. In Jesus' name, Amen!*

Why do you think you feel stuck?
(Ask God to help you get to the root.)

What have you tried to do on your own to change it?
(This will help you realize what failed so that you do not repeat.)

What are you expecting from God on this journey? *(We have not because we ask not; Be specific with God.)*

Journal your thoughts on the next page...

Unprocessed

Congratulations on embarking on this journey of self-development and healing. Today you should have clarity as to how you are fasting and are getting ready to or already have started. In the first two chapters I will share with you how I got to the point where God arrested my heart and began to do a new thing in me. This is in hopes that you begin to see yourself and be willing to go back to the depths of your personal story in order to confront the things that may have you stuck. My testimony is extensive but to give you some foundational history about me I will give you an expedited summary of some of the childhood traumas that I've endured.

One of my earliest memories at the age of five was being molested by my brother, who at the time was only eight and duplicated what happened to him. I remember it seemed like a game and when he was done, I stood up on the bed and was pretending as if I was writing on the wall. I began to sing, "I have a boyfriend!" "I have a boyfriend!" and my brother got up from where he was sitting and yelled, "No you don't! Don't say that!" That day I experienced hurt like I never knew; spiritually, I was introduced to perversion and rejection. The molestation happened one other time that I could remember and my mother, who had been molested herself as a child, responded by spanking us. I never wanted to see my mother angry, so for my 5-year-old self it was traumatic. The trauma response of freeze was my only option as I was too young for flight or fight, which are other types of common trauma responses.

As I got older, what I was shown and the things my body had experienced never went away. I knew it was wrong because that is what I was taught. What I wasn't taught was how to discuss what I felt. I wasn't taught how to unlearn the things that were presented to me and so I did what most kids do: When it happened again, this time from a kid in the neighborhood, I hid it. Then at some point I duplicated what was shown to me to other kids. The game of house became the norm and I always wanted to be the mommy because I would always manage to get alone time with the daddy. During these years I learned to be very sneaky, dishonest and almost anything I needed to be to avoid getting in trouble.

Around the age of eight, after a whole life of wondering what my father was like, I finally got to go and visit him. I had an older cousin that was present, and the molestation continued. At some point during this visit, my father's wife at the time cooked us a meal. This meal was foreign to me, so I remember telling him that I did not want to eat it. He was infuriated and told me that I was fat, and I needed to lose weight. Emotionally destroyed by his statement, my reply was, "I don't have to do anything but stay black and die." I then remember him saying that I was smart mouthed just like my mother. That night, he told us to pack our bags. The next morning, he checked them like a TSA agent and removed anything that we were given from the neighbor upstairs who left baked treats for us in the hall. He drove us back home and while he and his wife ate pizza, he fed us dry bologna sandwiches and water. He told us, "This is what they feed you in jail." That visit ended with even more rejection, perversion, and now self-esteem issues and an eating disorder.

This cycle continued up into my teenage years. It seemed to follow me. I remember even when we moved there was always some kid or another that would either touch me or I would touch them inappropriately and the never-ending game of house continued. There was even a moment where a girl showed me how there could be two mommies. So, these burdens I held on to in silence for years did a lot of damage that I was too young to even realize.

By the age of 13, I was wrapped in a lot of confusion. We were raised in church, but my mother stopped going at some point. Around that age, I began to take the church bus by myself to go. To my mother, it seemed like a good thing for a young girl to do. However, I went only because in school I was bullied but at church I had friends. Those friends were wrapped in the same confusion as me. We had youth leaders but needed more structure and transparent people leading to help us effectively. Church became a hang out spot and some of the things that went on between that group of friends right in the house of God is hard for me to even discuss. As a mentor and leader now, I will say to my fellow leaders and mentors, please know that if there is a will, the youth will make a way. From kissing, to touching, to fighting, to sex, when there is no structure or genuine teaching of the importance of a personal relationship with Christ, children/teens will act out on what the enemy throws at them.

> "To my fellow leaders and mentors, please know that if there is a will, the youth will make a way."

The age of 13 was a tough one for me so to sum it up, on the second visit to my father's house, I witnessed the abuse of his girlfriend, smoking, drinking, fighting, black eyes, bloodied hands, busted windows and a life I never knew in my home. I attributed all this chaos to me and a Christmas gift I wanted that he didn't want to get me, but his girlfriend got it anyway. So, I thought it was all my fault and I stayed up late to clean the mess. While trying to wash the dishes, I was sexually assaulted while standing at the sink by his friend's son, who was 19 and completely drunk. That led me to be confused because I didn't know if I was still a virgin or not. I repositioned myself when I felt the hurt of him forcing himself on me, to stop him from entering inside of me. Paralyzed by fear, nothing else came to mind. I couldn't even scream or fight. He didn't notice, so he continued until he released himself on my backside. That confusion caused me to seek out losing my virginity on my own terms once I got back home, which I later realized was a premature thought. I changed my mind while in the act and it was not received well by the other person. I ended up repositioning myself again to avoid conflict. Being the people pleaser that I had become, I sacrificed my own discomfort to appease someone else. This behavior is what would be the reason I would later make so many other bad decisions.

This is where things got worse, because I was taught incorrectly about intercourse. I thought a man releasing his fluids on me anywhere in my mid-section was enough to conceive. In my 13-year-old mind telling the truth wasn't an option. I partially thought I deserved what happened and for years didn't acknowledge what he had done as assault. So, to get medical help, I lied about being raped by a stranger in the alley some months later. The lying spirit rested upon me as a young child to cover all the games of house, but this one would be the one that haunted me and kept me bound for even more years. Another teaching moment: We must teach our children the truth. My mother was rather extreme with how she taught me about the birds and the bees. This did me more harm than good as I grew up.

Even as a grown woman, sharing these stories is not the most comfortable thing. However, I know my story is for the glory of God so I will speak it out so that more of my sisters and brothers in Christ can be set free. I once vowed I would never share with anyone the very things you've just read. That vow had to be renounced before I could even begin to heal. Now I ask you to go back into your own story. Ask the Holy Spirit to help you identify anything that could be holding you back or causing you to be stuck in your process. Be willing to look back even at some of the most hurtful things you have gone through. Once he reveals these things to you, write them down. Then pray this prayer...

Take a Minute to Pray and Process

*Heavenly Father God, I need you. I desire more of you, but I know there are places **(or reveal to me the places)** in my walk that are unpleasing to you. **(Be specific and call them out to God if you know them.)** God, please reveal the root of these things. If there is any place that needs to be healed, I ask that you heal me. Father, I desire more of you. Help me not to be afraid to face my past, but to boldly speak out about the things that may have had me stuck prohibiting me to go where you are calling me. In Jesus' name, Amen!*

Who hurt/disappointed you? *(Address the feelings that arise when you think of this person, and then give it to God.)*

Have you forgiven them and or yourself? *(Forgiveness is for you, not them.)*

How do you relate to what you just read?

Journal your thoughts on the next page...

Stuck in the Process

Processing

      In this chapter I will explain the part of my story that led me to write this book. Now that you know some of my traumas, you will now understand why the little girl in me made some of the decisions that were made. At this point I had still never spoken of the things that you read in the previous chapter, so I was very much so still in bondage. After the molestation was kind of swept under the rug as a child, I buried everything else deep inside also and tried to do what we too often are told to do: "be strong" and "press past it." This is what most hurt people were told to do in error. So, I feel led to take a moment and add that if your parent(s) made the mistake and sentenced you to silence, please take a moment to forgive her or his decisions made from their brokenness. *"If you forgive those who sin against you, your heavenly Father will forgive you. But if you refuse to forgive others, your Father will not forgive your sins."* (Matthew 6:14-15)

Now I want to make sure I say this point very clearly before we continue: This book is for individual healing and growth. I will reference my marriage a lot because that is what caused my breaking point. My soul being healed and saved was the mission, but my marriage being saved was a byproduct of that. Each of us has different things that challenge us so you may not relate to the fact that my marriage is how I discovered my need for growth, but the key point is growth and God can use any relationship or situation you are in to teach you the very lessons that I will share in the next chapters. My pastor always says, "Chew the meat and spit out the bone." So, if you cannot relate to the experiences I've had, please ask the Holy Spirit to show you how the lessons are applicable to your story.

I was 19 when I met my husband; it was shortly after I left home at the age of 18. I had no preparation to be out on my own but wanted nothing more than to leave home, so I did! I found a program that allowed me to leave without the help of my family. That took me from my hometown of Detroit to Chicago, which is where I met my husband. Our story was whimsical to be honest. Our relationship started so organically that even our residential advisor said that we were going to make it. We were both packaged pretty, so in no time we went from friends to lovers. I was on this campus for a year and a half, and I managed to stay away from dating anyone. My goal was to get to know myself; dating was the last thing on my mind. He came and within a week or two I was in a relationship! It's okay to laugh. He clearly swept me off my feet. I don't know if it was his transparency, us praying every night together, or the fact that he wrote me these beautiful letters proclaiming Jesus as Lord and me as his wife, but one thing was certain I wasn't ready to let go even when I tried.

Our story began in Chicago, and led us to Columbus, Ohio. We took many faith leaps because we first trusted God and second were two people who felt we had nothing to lose and everything to gain from leaving the places where we were raised. However, we were still two very broken individuals. I wanted nothing more than to be a trophy wife. From the time we met I spoiled him as he did me. The problem was

> **The problem was that our perception of love wasn't realistic or sustainable.**

Processing

that our perception of love wasn't realistic or sustainable.

My husband had a very hard life; he practically has been on his own since he was 16. His father was a drug addict, and his mother was a very broken single mother. Her ways of disciplining her children were not the healthiest ways to say the least. My husband has experienced a life riddled with gang violence, drugs, addiction, and he too was introduced to the spirit of perversion at a very young age. He has dealt with rejection, betrayal, and deep hurt from people that he once loved and trusted with his life. His story would make this book as lengthy as an encyclopedia, but please be on the lookout for it soon! Everything he endured caused him to be very unempathetic, selfish, and angry. Now I must say this, my husband was very transparent with me about his life's failures and achievements. I walked into our relationship knowing all the hurt he endured, but I was too blinded by my hurt to realize that we would soon begin to clash. The people pleaser in me did what people pleasers do. I made everything about him and required little from him and as the broken man, he allowed it. We created a very one-sided relationship.

Before we knew it, we had children and were beginning to realize how different we were. I would say a lot of our issues were "swept under the rug" so to speak. I remember beginning to feel as if I couldn't talk to him because our discussions would always end in an argument. I remember one argument between the two of us where we broke a new game system, a new T.V, and a few other things. We had no clue how to communicate, much less work through our differences.

It would be impossible to get to the point of this book with every detail of the things we have endured being listed but after years of lack of communication, acting out of brokenness, church hurt, backsliding and immaturity, we endured adultery, relapse and separation. I can honestly say that it is only by the grace of God that we are still standing. We both agree that if one of us had been healed before the other we would not have made it because neither of us deserved the broken version of each other that we had. God was faithful enough to us to not let us end up as the villain of each other's story. We healed while still together and have been able to help each other heal through this journey called life.

> Therefore, when people say "It's my truth," it's a very dangerous thing to say. "Your truth" is not "The Truth."

However, before God healed us, we had to deal with the issues that we swept under the rug. I had become someone who embraced the victim mindset. A lot of the things I did were reactions to the things that he did. So, I would blame him for everything as if I was not in control of my own actions regardless of what he did. I also became self-righteous. I got to a place where I based what I did off of what I used to do. Therefore, when people say, "It's my truth," it's a very dangerous thing to say. "Your truth" is not "The Truth." What God says goes and that is all. It's easy to get caught up in justifying who you are by who you were and that is not what God calls us to do. The Bible says, *"throw off your old sinful nature and your former way of life, which is corrupted by lust and deception. Instead, let the Spirit renew your thoughts and attitudes. Put on your new nature, created to be like God-truly righteous and holy."* (Ephesians 4:22-24)

We got to a place where we were both growing and seeking God individually and very active in our church. However, every time something from the past came up it was like we were reliving it. A woman from his past found out some information about our current church home and life ventures and made sure I was aware; it immediately took me back. Since our history of communicating was so bad, us talking about how she knew led to an argument. I began to deal with the attack of the enemy on my thoughts. My husband has a lot of habits that are peculiar and those became the catalyst that the enemy would use to confirm the things that were in my thoughts. The enemy will not only plant seeds but send people and things to water them if you don't recognize it's him. I began to feel the need to communicate with someone about all my mixed emotions. At this time, I still struggled with what I now know was pride. I didn't want to talk to anyone that knew my husband because I didn't want people to know that our marriage was as damaged as it was. I had yet to learn that we are to protect our spouses but not to the point where we are suffering in silence.

Communication was something we struggled with before we separated but even more so after we decided to make our marriage work. The exposure I had to other people who were better communicators, and the emotional attachments that were created, became a challenge for me. During our time of separation, I made several of those connections thinking it was harmless. I now know it was selfish gain and very harmful. This was where it all came back to bite me in the butt. I went back into old ways seeking comfort from someone who I thought was a Godly man. This person I had known for a little while, and I blindly didn't see that he was attracted to me. I decided one day to give him a call and literally just seek his advice and counsel. I can't say that I didn't know it was wrong to speak to another man about my marriage. It was just familiar from the past, and I wrongfully made the decision. Within the first call, it was very clear that we were both going through trying times and he saw me differently than I had ever expected. After learning this I should have never spoken to him again but in all truth, it was flattering. My immature ways and the body shaming that I inwardly struggled with since I was eight, (due to me holding on to my father's words and being overweight,) made me count myself out as his type. Second, he knew how to converse in a way that made me feel heard. These interactions happened for a week or so and then I found myself not only counting my marriage out as done with, but wondering if there was someone better. I looked up and found myself back in a very familiar mindset and was ready to ruin everything we had all because someone opened my thoughts to "better" and "easier" from somewhere else. The crazy part is it wasn't that person that I wanted those things with, but they planted the seed of desire to find easier and less complicated elsewhere. The enemy can and will use anyone and when you aren't healed in an area, you have a blind spot to it. I was so tired of repeating our inability to communicate and the petty arguments. I wanted nothing more than peace even if that meant ending our marriage. This quick instance of a few bad decisions turned me right back to my old way of thinking, and there I was for a moment, dipping my toe in the water of who I used to be.

> **The enemy can and will use anyone and when you aren't healed in an area, you have a blind spot to it.**

That situation for us was yet again one of too many swept under the rug. It led to a big argument at a church small group that earned us a trip to our pastor's office. For the first time in our marriage, we began to receive counseling that was long overdue. As they asked me about what happened with this person I confided in, I saw no error. I literally believed that since I did not do what I would have done in the past and I had ended the inappropriate communications months prior, that there was nothing wrong. I believed that our biggest issues came from years prior and that I would make sure they knew that what I did was justified by his ways. Man, I had a messed-up mindset!

I went to the meeting prepared for them to tell my husband that he was wrong, he was mean, full of pride and anger and that he did not spiritually cover me and our children properly. I was looking for justification to not have to do work but to leave the chaos that we created. I guess at this place in my life I was embracing the trauma response of flight. It seemed easier to just leave than stay and fight. The spirits of self-righteousness, pride, and lust had me blinded to "The Truth" as I was living out "my truth."

That meeting ended up being all about me. It's not that my husband's ways and errors weren't a factor, but God just didn't address them at this point. I was at a place where had I died, my soul might have been condemned to hell. I had unforgiveness, pride, self-righteousness, and my heart had been hardened in areas. Even though I was in the church, tithing, and genuinely changing I was not surrendering the inner depths of me. I didn't know how to surrender those

> **I was at a place where had I died, my soul might have been condemned to hell.**

things or felt a need to; but like a good father, God helped me to see me. It was a long three hours of me denying and deflecting before I faced the truth, but that day God used my husband and my pastor in a way that broke off years of childhood trauma. In the midst of exposure, being crushed, and feeling low, God used them to show me love in the way that only He can. To be shown undeserving love from these two men in one of my lowest hours was a breaking point for me. It was a moment that God restored and loved His daughter in the way that my earthly father was unable to do. It felt like years of rebellion and hurt were taken away and I was finally able to see myself in the way that God sees me.

There is no "place" that we reach in Christ where we are not going to fight against the desire to sin. Our goal is to die daily, to seek God's face daily and to read our word and pray daily. I had changed as much as I could on my own, this part had to be done by God. After this experience, God led me to do the puzzle that I spoke about in the beginning of this book. This is where God showed me how to combat the years of bad decisions due to trauma. He lovingly showed me how to process the process. I didn't know that I was impatient with the process and that I had no clue how to embrace it because it would mean I would need to unlearn so many things. What process is this, you ask? It is the process of healing and sanctification because you really can't obtain one without the other.

Take a Minute to Pray and Process

Father, today I seek your face for guidance in the dying-to-self process. Help me to see the things that have kept me bound and unable to begin to truly be grafted into the tree of life. Help me Father to acknowledge my ugly ways. **(If you know what you battle, be specific. If not ask him to reveal it.)** *Help me to put down all old habits no matter the circumstances around me. Today I acknowledge that I am in control of my actions no matter what hurtful things anyone else does or says to me. Today I ask that you break down every wall that I have built internally to protect me; I give full protection of me to you because only in your arms am I safe. Help me to trust you in this very vulnerable state as I will look to you for how to react in order to stop the cycle that has yielded me nothing. Lord, help me to also forgive myself, and where you are removing things like pride from me, please replace them with their opposites like humility, gratitude, and joy. I thank you; I trust you, and I will embrace the process that you have set before me. In Jesus' name, Amen!*

How did you relate to this chapter?

How did it make you feel?

Were you reminded of anything in your own life?

Journal your thoughts on the next page...

Stuck in the Process

Process of Sanctification
(The Life Cycle of a Butterfly)

God began to show me that our walk with Christ is very similar to the process a butterfly goes through in its life cycle; it happens in phases. Even though our salvation is instantaneous, our flesh must unlearn a lot of things that we have become accustomed to, which is the process of sanctification. If we don't embrace change just as naturally as a caterpillar embraces its change to become a butterfly, we become stuck in our process.

After I came to the end of my self, where I realized that doing things my way was not working, I finally surrendered. I stopped picking and choosing where I would say yes to God and began to allow Him in to even the deepest of places in my heart. I allowed the seed of salvation to take root and the birthing of a new woman to begin. I no longer tried to make God fit into my life but allowed Him to take full control. Now the process could truly progress!

Next you will read the 10 processes that the Holy Spirit showed me to help me become unstuck in my process of healing and sanctification. Each process had to be applied over the course of a year. The Holy Spirit truly preceded me and made sure I had everything that I needed to begin to unlearn my old ways and embrace the new ways.

Process 1: Put God First

After being confronted with the things I buried, God led me to complete a puzzle that I bought a month prior. I have not completed a puzzle in my adult life, but while shopping with the family I grabbed this puzzle, honestly, because it was on sale and the box was pretty. Well at least I thought! Leading up to me starting, I began to buy things for the puzzle like a mat and sorting bins. It was all foreign to me, but I was sure in my spirit that I needed to work on it, so I was obedient.

On day one I worked so diligently to separate all the end pieces. I got the bulk of them together after a few hours and soon realized I was missing three pieces. I remember being so frustrated. How did I go through all of this for three pieces to be missing? I went through the leftover pieces at least three times. My children even went through them, but we saw nothing. I walked away that day so frustrated and confused. I thought, "Why did I feel so led to do this puzzle and I won't even be able to complete it without the framework being whole?"

I made up my mind that it was garbage and that I must've got something wrong. I began to question the leading of the Holy Spirit wondering if I got it wrong. After resting and talking to God I felt the need to go back through the pieces on the next day. I immediately found two of the missing pieces. This was my first download from God. He showed me that on my own strength I got burned out and tired, but when I rested in Him the puzzle pieces began to fall into place, "pun intended." *"Then Jesus said, 'Come to me all of you who are weary and carry heavy burdens, and I will give you rest. Take my yoke upon you. Let me teach you, because I am humble and gentle at heart, and you will find rest for your souls. For my yoke is easy to bear, and the burden I give you is light.'"* (Matthew 11:28-30)[1]

Then as I sought out the last piece, it seemed to be the hardest of them all. I was beginning to get frustrated again; I realized that the one piece was needed for a complete foundation or again, "This puzzle is trash!" I proclaimed. God then showed me that our lives without Him are as worthless as the frame to my puzzle. Without a complete frame—a firm foundation—life is unstable, and harder to live.

> **God showed me that every failure, every issue, repetitively battled, was all due to me making Him the last piece of my decisions.**

I was guilty of trying to fill the voids of my heart and broken marriage with other people, ministry, business, and even my children. God showed me that every failure, every issue, repetitively battled, was all due to me making Him the last piece of my decisions. I, like many of you, would make up my mind that something was going to work because I wanted it, then ask God to bless it, instead of seeking God first and building upon His yes.

The Bible says, *"Seek ye first the kingdom of God, and his righteousness; and all these things shall be added unto you."* (Matthew 6:33)[2] I'm a visual learner and when I do things hands on, the lesson sticks with me so, for me, this puzzle made sense. God had to show me what we look like every time we try to build outside of Him. All the frustrations that I dealt with in life could have been avoided had I not built almost to completion and then asked God to help as a last resort. When my husband's and my relationship started, it was truly built on us putting God first (at least to the extent we knew how to). At some point, that stopped. We began to be led by our emotions and once the words that couldn't be taken back were said we would ask God to fix it. If only we would have put Him first! Let us pray!

Take a Minute to Pray and Process

Father God, today I ask that you transform my mind to think of you before anything or anyone else. Help me to remember that you are all that matters in this life and without you everything I do is meaningless. God, I thank you for loving me flaws and all, and not leaving me in the places that I have outgrown. Help me to identify the things that I have built up on my own strength and then expected you to bless. Help me to dismantle anything that you have not given me for I know it is just a distraction from the things for which you have created me. Forgive me for not seeking you first in things **(call it out)** _____. *I give this to you and will no longer carry this as an idol in my heart. You can have all of me. In Jesus' name, Amen!*

In what area(s) have you failed to put God first?
How did reading this lesson make you feel?
What was your takeaway from this process?
Journal your thoughts on the next page...

Stuck in the Process

 *Chapter 4*

Process 2: Let God Lead the Way

As the week progressed and I worked more on this puzzle, I found myself getting overwhelmed. I decided that I wanted to work on two or three different areas of the puzzle so that I didn't get bored. I had three different piles of three different colors sorted out on the table in front of me. Looking back at it, it was a chaotic workspace. It became so complex that I found myself not wanting to finish the puzzle. I also slowed down my progress because once I couldn't find a piece to lay in one area I just moved to the next, which made things worse because all I kept doing was going in a circle and giving very little effort to each individual area. The big picture seemed too far away, and I began to doubt if I could ever complete this thousand-piece puzzle.

Then I got my next download. God showed me that I needed to choose one area to dedicate my time and efforts to first. As I began to do things His way, it seemed to just flow. The key is, I, exercising my free will, had to choose to do things His way. God is a gentleman; He gives us the choice. My way of doing things caused me to give less than my best. We have gotten so accustomed to variety that we are so quick to jump around versus commit to one thing at a time.

God leading me into this process was to reveal to me that I did not know how to process things, and this day was proof that I had no clue. My life was a similitude of how I tried to finish this puzzle. I would try to tackle fixing everything at one time. I wanted God to fix my husband. Remember at one point in my mind, he was the issue. I wanted him to fix me and fix my marriage among other things. What I really needed to do was focus on me. Everything in my life is a bonus but what God cares about most is our soul. Once I began to pray and ask God to heal me, to expose me, and show me where I needed to change, everything else began to fall into place.

The next thing is, whoever said that the grass is greener on the other side was not very truthful! Just like I was ready to jump from pile to pile and color to color, that's how most of us are in our lives, job to job, relationship to relationship, etc. It's truly a mental conditioning that will fail us. I was ready to move on because from childhood I was conditioned to options and an easy way out mentality. Please know the grass isn't greener on the other side. It is greener where you water and fertilize it. This is why choosing one thing to work on at a time matters so much; you will be focused and less likely to get distracted. Let us pray!

> **Please know the grass isn't greener on the other side. It is greener where you water and fertilize it.**

Take a Minute to Pray and Process

Heavenly Father God, thank you for loving me so much that even though I can come as I am you will not leave me where I am. Thank you for being so gracious in showing me a road map to healing and restoration. Today, Father I ask that you give me clarity on what part of my life that I need to yield to you first. Help me to put down the things that are causing me to be confused and therefore unproductive. I pray that I hear you clearly and see the blueprint that you have for my life. Help me God to be effective to do what you have purposed me to do. God help me to see what I am doing that may be good but not Godly. I only want to move in what you have called for me to move in. Father God lead me out of any confusion that I may have in my business, ministry, marriage, family, and overall, my life. Today I surrender it all to you and what you lead me to let go I will let go. Give me strength, Father, to get out of my own way and to adopt your way. In Jesus' name, Amen.

In what area(s) have you failed to let God lead?
How did reading this lesson make you feel?
What did you take away from this process?
Journal your thoughts on the next page...

Stuck in the Process

Process 3: Don't Get Distracted

The next lesson came as I got to a place where I thought I had the swing of things. I was getting used to the puzzle and seemed to be making traction on the road to completion. Then I came across what I called an "Imposter Piece." This piece was the right color; it was even the right shape, because it fit the spot that I had it in, but it did not belong. After learning to focus on one area in my last process, I was able to quickly realize that there was an issue. I had a thought to just go back to another area again, but I listened to God and stuck with the one area even when things began to seem stuck. This helped me to identify what the issue was rather quickly. I began to look closely at the area and found that there was a line that did not match. I removed the piece and just like that everything began to flow again. Had I been disobedient I would have gone backwards and prolonged the process of finding the issue.

> **The reality of it is, no matter how much we love our spouses we cannot change them. That is God's job.**

In my marriage, this was my battle with control. Trying to "fix things" myself made me the imposter because God does not need our help. I wanted God to fix my husband so badly that I didn't keep my eyes on me, regardless of the things that were happening around me. The reality of it is, no matter how much we love our spouses we cannot change them.

That is God's job. One of the hardest lessons was learning that regardless of what my husband did or did not do I am responsible for me and me alone. If you love someone give the person back to their Creator and He will do what is needed for things to work for His good.

I spent a lot of time going before the Lord, and thinking I was humbling myself to do His will, until my husband would do or say something that triggered me and yet again, I would be distracted with things I couldn't control. This left me taking things back into my own hands and living in confusion. Had I stayed focused on the one area that God wanted me to focus on which was me, I would have been able to see the works of the enemy rather quickly. The word says, *"And why do you look at the speck in your brother's eye, but do not consider the plank in your own eye? Or how can you say to your brother, 'Let me remove the speck from your eye', and look, a plank in your own eye? Hypocrite! First remove the plank from your own eye, and then you will see clearly to remove the speck from your brother's eye."* (Matthew 7:3-5)[3]

> **...the imposter was the enemy within me.**

Just like in my puzzle lesson, my focus, against all odds, should have been where God led me, and He would have shown me the imposter was the enemy within me. The war was not between my husband and I, but between the spiritual forces that we allowed to work through us. The enemy does not like it when you have decided to fight your battles the correct way. The only time that he trembles is when we fight back in the spiritual realm. He will influence any and every one that is available to get you to stop. Keep your eyes on Jesus! Distractions are one of the enemy's greatest tools to stop us from walking into our destiny. Let us pray!

Take a Minute to Pray and Process

Abba Father, help me to identify any distractions that may be keeping me from doing what you have told me to do. Help me to identify the "imposter pieces", the relationships, business ventures, etc. that are keeping me from doing what you called me to do. Help me to keep my eyes set upon you. No matter what people say or do, help me to remember that I stand before you alone on judgement day. Help me, Father, to be strong enough to stand on your word even when all odds seem to be against me. Help me to remember that when I seek vengeance that I am stealing from you for you said "Beloved, do not avenge yourselves, but rather give place to wrath; for it is written, 'Vengeance is Mine, I will repay,' says the Lord." (Romans 12:19)[4] You are my protector, and you will cover me in all ways. I trust you and I will allow you to fight my battles. I thank you in advance because I know that it is done! In Jesus' name, Amen!

What or who is a distraction in your life?

How did reading this lesson make you feel?

What did you take away from this process?

Journal your thoughts on the next page...

Stuck in the Process

Process 3: Don't Get Distracted

Phase 1:
Our Yes (The Egg)

The egg is one of the most delicate phases of the butterfly's life. There is a special fluid that holds the eggs to the plant on which they are born. This fluid protects them from danger[4]. For us, that special fluid is the blood of Jesus, and the plant is the tree of life. After we commit our yes to salvation, going back to a childlike state is challenging but necessary.

"Assuredly, I say to you, unless you are converted and become as little children, you will by no means enter the kingdom of heaven." (Matthew 18:3)[5]

The three previous processes you just read are key in this phase. We must put God first, let Him lead, and not allow distractions to cause us to go backwards. It does not matter what you have done in your past, you are covered by the blood of Jesus and are considered a new creation in Christ. *"Therefore, if anyone is in Christ, he is a new creation; old things have passed away; behold, all things have become new. Now all things are of God, who has reconciled us to Himself through Jesus Christ, and has given us the ministry of reconciliation, that is, that God was in Christ reconciling the world to Himself, not imputing their trespasses to them, and has committed to us the word of reconciliation."* (2 Corinthians 5:17-19)[6]

Process 4: Press In

I had to be a few weeks into my puzzle, and I got to a place where I was stuck yet again. I was just sure that it was another imposter piece somewhere because of my prior experience. However, I paused to ask God this time and I felt the nudge in my spirit to apply pressure. I called this piece a "Pressure Piece". God began to show me how we learn from our experiences, but not everything is going to be a repeat.

In my marriage, the social media notifications that showed me that the lady from my husband's past was lurking on our pages took me into a place of "not this again." I hadn't healed, so I immediately went into me protecting myself again. What I was supposed to do was press in harder to God; to trust that if there was anything going on, that He would reveal it to me. Over the course of this puzzle, God continuously showed me things. It was His way of reminding me that I hear Him. It's the same for you too. We must remember that a loving father will always speak, we just need to listen. Often, just like in my case, our traumas speak louder than Him and we find ourselves in these ridiculous cycles. I was literally on my way back to the very place that I once begged God to deliver me from, all for a misunderstanding that the enemy used for his agenda to destroy. *"Be sober, be vigilant, because your adversary the devil walketh about as a roaring lion, seeking whom he may devour."* (1 Peter 5:8) [7]

Stuck in the Process

This is why we need to have a relationship with God and when we feel like something is wrong, press in and trust Him to lead you through. I know when the situation is as sensitive as a marriage, we can tend to move based on our emotions. It would be remiss of me to not tell you that sometimes your feelings need to be rebuked. If what you feel does not align with the word of God, then you are in error. Ask God what is triggering you so that you can address the root of the issue. I was guilty of thinking that I was justified in doing something in response to something my husband did, but I was wrong. What I was called to do was to press in and trust God even when things didn't make sense. Instead, I reacted based on past hurt.

Our individual growth and healing is so important. Had I been healed, my reaction would not have been to protect myself with my own strength, it would have been to sit at the feet of Jesus and get even lower in his presence. *"Fear not, for I am with you; Be not dismayed, for I am your God. I will strengthen you, Yes, I will help you, I will uphold you with My righteous right hand."* (Isaiah 41:10)[8] You do not have to worry about protecting yourself, just keep trusting and pressing into God. Let us pray...

Take a Minute to Pray and Process

Heavenly Father God, I ask that you help me to remember that in my weakness you are made strong. Today, no matter what my issues are, I choose you. No matter what things look like around me, Father, I will stand on your Word and trust your promises. God help me to desire more time in your presence. Help me God to seek you before I allow anything from my past to trigger me. God, move on my behalf and as I seek you, God, reveal to me all that needs to be seen. Father, because I know the enemy is sneaky, I ask that you also guard my heart. If what you show me is something I see differently from you, help me to remember that you are still good, and your way is best. I thank you Father for your love and mercy and today and every day moving forward, Father, I vow to press in more and more. In Jesus' name, Amen.

How will you press in?

How did reading this lesson make you feel?

What did you take away from this process?

Journal your thoughts on the next page...

Stuck in the Process

Process 5: Walk by Faith, Not by Sight

This next piece I called a Transition Piece. I was working in the now "one area" of my choosing and I began to realize that there seemed to be pieces missing. I had only a few of that color left and none of them seemed to fit. I soon realized it was because I was looking for the wrong thing. The pieces that I had belonged to another part of the puzzle that were the exact same color. The puzzle was transitioning, and I didn't realize it because I was looking for the same thing that I had been working on the whole time.

This is what happens when God begins to do a new thing in our lives: it happens suddenly. When God showed me this, I began to reflect on how we like to seek what's comfortable because the unknown is uncomfortable. When God began to heal my marriage, I had to be solely dependent upon Him. God wanted to show me new things and I, for a while, kept holding on to the old things. It's hard to see things the way that God wants you to when you are so busy trying to stay in control. Your next level is not in your comfort zone or under your control. It is where God wants to take you but only He knows when the season will change. It is a fact that you cannot experience God and not be changed.

God showed me where I made my marriage an idol in my heart. I had a fear of losing it because, first, I loved my husband in an unhealthy way. Being intimate before marriage created an unhealthy soul tie that I later had to renounce. Second, I had a fear of generational curses being carried out and my children not having both parents. That was a problematic thought process because children raised in an unhealthy toxic environment

> ...children raised in an unhealthy toxic environment with two parents is more damaging than it is good.

with two parents is more damaging than it is good. So, my transition was learning that I had to be willing to let my marriage go. I had to give it to God completely for it to be healed and for healthy boundaries to be created.

I remember the day that God led me to have the conversation with my husband pertaining to the things he showed me about our marriage. I was honestly apprehensive to say the least, but I had faith in God. I couldn't allow what I had seen in the past from my husband when dealing with situations like this to stop us from having this talk. God literally ushered us into the conversation because on my husband's way home from work that day he had a near-death experience. He was so full of gratitude and joy that I almost felt like I would ruin his mood. We went on a family ride and afterwards I dropped our children off at home. I was asking God the whole time, "If it is meant to be, please give us time alone, away from our children." That is exactly what ended up happening! After they were dropped off at home, my husband stayed in the car with me, parked in our driveway, and said "Can we just sit and talk for a while?" God is faithful in that way!

I had no clue how my husband would react to hearing about our unhealthy soul tie and my willingness to let go and let God but what I did know is that I had to be obedient. There weren't many times in my marriage that I would put my foot down and demand to be heard, but this was one of those times. This transition was needed, and the conversation went better than I could have ever imagined.

He heard me, and instead of getting angered he felt so much remorse for the things that I have endured by his hand. He began to understand how that guy that got in my ear was able to do so. He finally saw me after 18 years of marriage. The broken little girl that never healed got to cry out to the man that couldn't see she existed because of the pedestal that he put her on. Our marriage transitioned that night and our healing journey had begun.

Take a Minute to Pray and Process

Heavenly Father God, I want to thank you for my life and everything that I often overlook thanking you for. Thank you for transitioning me to higher heights and deeper depths in you. You are Alpha and Omega and I know that you alone know what is best for me. Help me in transitions to seek you, and to see your hands on my life even when I am uncomfortable. Help me God to embrace the changes that are required for me to grow in you. Today, God, I ask that your will be done in my life. I ask father, that anything in me that has become an idol in my heart is revealed so that I can renounce it and relinquish it to you. Help me, Father, see from a kingdom perspective. I thank and love you. In Jesus' name, Amen.

In what areas have you lost faith?

How did reading this lesson make you feel?

What did you take away from this process?

Journal your thoughts on the next page...

Stuck in the Process

Process 6: Heart Posture

It had to be about a month into the puzzle at this point and I realized that I had a heart posture change. When I first started working on this puzzle, I was confused but I knew that I needed to do it, so I was reluctantly obedient. This particular day I found myself excited to make my way downstairs to my workstation. I remember preparing for the time that I would take to work on the puzzle. There was a sense of joy that overtook me, and I went to finish working on my assignment.

I worked on the puzzle and allowed my mind to be clear waiting to hear another word from the Lord. It wasn't until I was finished working for the day that he began to show me that my heart posture had changed. Instead of doing it out of just obedience I did it out of delight and desire. I wanted to do it because in the weeks prior I had learned that what He wants for me is what is best. It may have seemed silly and sometimes I did wonder if I was crazy. At one point I even reached out to my pastor telling him about my experience and asking, "Is this what the Bible means when it says, *'But God has chosen the foolish things of the world to put to shame the wise, and God has chosen the weak things of the world to put to shame the things which are mighty'*" (1 Cor 1:27)[9] My pastor replied, "God has a way to reach us all in the way that we will learn best."

My marriage and my walk with God looked very similar in one way. When I felt like fighting harder, I did and when I didn't feel like it, well, I didn't. It was easier to just default to what I knew best, not allowing myself to feel my emotions. I needed a serious change in my heart posture. I needed to allow God to love me so that I could fully love my husband.

One of the first steps to break this cycle was God taking my love for worship music and replacing it with a love to hear sermons from a pastor that He led me to. After a while I wanted more of His word, so I began to listen to my Bible on a Bible app. From there I began to grab pen and paper because I wanted to study and cross-reference things. I grew into loving the word of God just like I grew into wanting to complete my puzzle.

> **I wept realizing that no matter what my husband had done my posture was to remain that of a wife.**

God showed me that the damage we had caused one another in our marriage had made me numb. I was quickly ready to just let it go anytime we had to deal with unresolved issues of our past. God showed me that before I was my husband's wife, I was a part of the church, which is the bride of Christ. (Ephesians 5:22-27) He also began to lead me to the story of Hosea and Gomer and how that was His love story with His people. I wept realizing that no matter what my husband had done my posture was to remain that of a wife. He then lovingly showed me that my adulterous ways were to Him first. This was the defining moment for me; this revelation changed my life.

Looking back at our whole story, the fact that God used my husband as he did Hosea to redeem his bride literally brings me to tears. He loves me so much that He allowed me to experience the ultimate type of love, an Agape love. I did not deserve to be met after our meeting with our pastor

Process 6: Heart Posture

with so much love from my husband. However, that is a type of love that God knew I had never known and never thought existed. It's the type of love that He has for us all.

That experience was the catalyst for what God used to change my heart posture for my husband. The meeting with our pastor was just the beginning of a new process. The old things I endured were still very prevalent in our marriage, but God made sure I saw for myself that my husband was a man submitted to Him. That gave me the hope that I had once lost. So now when things would arise that would trigger me, I learned to fight for my husband and not with him. I began to pray for our marriage instead of operating in my flight or freeze trauma responses. My heart changed and the renewed love God gave me for my husband could only be described as supernatural. Because of this, I began to pray differently and when attacks of the past would come, I learned to not feed into the madness but to step back and see the attack as what it really was: the enemy seeking to destroy our marriage.

In our walk of sanctification, the heart posture shift is one of the biggest changes. It's when we learn to unlearn all the characteristic defaults that we have become accustomed to. We truly begin to love what God loves and hate what God hates. Doing what is required of us as Sons and Daughters of God becomes our biggest delight.

Take a Minute to Pray and Process

Today, God, I thank you for a heart transformation. Show me the places in my heart that have become numb or cold. Heal me from all hurt and reveal to me the things that do harm me, but I have buried to avoid feeling the pain. Father, I ask that You allow me to delight in You above all else. Change my desires, change my will and emotions to be the vessel that You have created me to be. Today, Abba I choose to forgive all who have trespassed against me. Help me, God, to release all tension, pain, and unresolved issues to you. You said that I can cast all cares unto You and today, that is what I choose to do. Help me, Father, to replace these feelings and emotions with your Word, your love, your peace, and your presence. Give me a new heart and replace my heart of stone. In Jesus' name, Amen.

What does Heart Posture mean to you?

How did reading this lesson make you feel?

What did you take away from this process?

Journal your thoughts on the next page...

Process 6: Heart Posture

Stuck in the Process

Phase 2:
Servitude (The Caterpillar)

The caterpillar's number one job is to eat. They often start with the very leaf where they were born[10]. I found this to be quite fascinating because the Bible says that we are not to live by bread alone, but by every word that proceeds from the mouth of God. (Matthew 4:4) Our job when we receive Jesus as our Lord and Savior is to read (eat) of His word so that we can know who He is and who we are in Him. It is beyond important for us to eat of the word of God in our beginning stages. His word will be the foundation on which we stand as trials and tribulations come.

This phase is where the previous three processes will be needed most. First, when reading the Bible seems hard, press in. Second, when you read, believe and walk in it by faith. Last, let your heart be changed by the words that are written in God's word. This also means that we will need to change what we allow into our ear and eye gates. If we don't guard ourselves, falling back into old habits, as you can see in my story, is very likely.

Process 7: Continue to Choose His Way

While putting this puzzle together, God had given me so many confirmations that I was not crazy or over spiritualizing this experience. So, once I was confident in this, I began to look forward to it, so much so that I would want to go and sit to work on the puzzle even at times that I should be doing other things. This is one of the moments that God had to show me how badly I liked to rush the process. I was willing to change the process in order to get it done quicker. Clearly there is no rushing a puzzle, so spending more time on it to get it done was the only way. God had to show me the order of operation, basically, and even gave me a window to work. How could I be willing to take time away from my family? How could I sacrifice the things that are first for something that could honestly wait, even though God gave it to me to complete? I had to remember that His timing is better than mine and that being patient with the process was important.

This had been me with my walk in my ministry and my marriage. God would show me something and I would bend over backwards to get it done, trying to get to the end result. This meant even if it included taking time away from other God-given duties or if it took away from my alone time with God I would mistakenly give it precedence. God ministered to me and showed me that

> **God ministered to me and showed me that the assignment should never come before the assignor...**

the assignment should never come before the assignor, and it definitely can't come before the natural order that He has given us for our lives.

This assignment had become very important for me to complete, but not at the cost of taking time away from my family, or even my alone time in the presence of God. This process began to show me the difference between good and God. I would often get so caught up in doing a good thing that the things that God really had set out for me to do were overlooked. I was addicted to being busy. God in this process graciously showed me how there was a root issue to my need-for-speed thought process. The real issues were the things in my marriage that weren't addressed. Instead of remembering His word, I would want to move on to the next thing. Well sometimes the only way to move forward is to go back to the last thing God told us. We must make a mindful decision throughout our journey to continue choosing His way.

After this process was revealed to me, I had to face the reality that I allowed ministry, and everyone attached to the ministry to take precedence over my marriage. This is not how God intends for us to live. Often, we can get caught up doing things in ministry outside of the home not realizing that our home is our first calling. *"One who rules his own house well, having his children in submission with all reverence (for if a man does not know how to rule his own house, how will he take care of the church of God?)"* (1Timothy 3:4-5)[11] I was guilty of a few things but the main two were allowing the hit of dopamine that we get from doing good to keep me blinded to my inner issues and living a life out of God's order.

Process 7: Continue to Choose His Way

I had to learn to choose God's way no matter what. I had to learn to no longer allow issues to be swept under the rug to become a better steward of my own home. The Bible says, *"But if anyone does not provide for his own, and especially for those of his household, he has denied the faith and is worse than an unbeliever."* (1Tim 5:8)[12] My home being out of order was the representation of my real fruit, not the outward "good" that was portrayed at the church. My reality was I had bad fruit, we had bad fruit, and it was time to let God fix our mess.

I was led to no longer tell my husband, "I don't care" or "It is what it is." God showed me how these phrases were not only lies but they were stumbling blocks for my husband. I had to learn to submit when led to submit but stand firm when led to stand firm. In our situation, my husband had a lot of growing to do as well, so often God used me to show him new things just like He used him to show me new things. Talking about the things we will no longer do that caused each other pain in the past was essential to our growth. The enemy would still try to pin us against one another, but I was equipped with the process that God gave me and I knew that no matter what I had to choose God's way. So, when my husband would do things that took me back to an unhappy place, I would remind myself that I'm no longer allowing his actions to dictate my actions. I had to have a made-up mind that I would continue to choose God's way. My doing this allowed my husband to truly see the God in me. As time progressed, he began to act less like the old and embraced the new.

Take a Minute to Pray and Process

Heavenly Father God, thank you for reminding me that your way is the only way that leads to true freedom. Thank you for allowing me to take ownership of my actions no matter what is said or done to me. Help me to not allow my actions to be constant reactions to other people actions. Today I ask that you open my eyes and allow me to see myself; help me see areas of improvement. Help me to let the God I know be the God that I show to people who meet me. I do not want to continue to lean on my own understanding but have complete trust in your process. Today I declare that I will stop to pray before reacting, at work, at home, with my spouse, with my children, with my parents, or anyone that I come across. I want my ways to be pleasing to your sight, oh, God. Help me to remember to continue to put you first! In Jesus' name, Amen!

How will you be intentional about continuously choosing Gods way?

How did reading this lesson make you feel?

What did you take away from this process?

Journal your thoughts on the next page...

Process 7: Continue to Choose His Way

Chapter 10

Process 8: Know His Voice

My delight for this process had begun to overtake my thoughts. I wanted so badly to not over-spiritualize this that I began to do just that. I finished one whole side of the puzzle and there was one piece missing, dead center that side. I began to look around for this piece going through all the others just to not find it. So, I asked "Ohhhh! What is this lesson?", excited to understand what the missing center piece meant. I got in my own head and I'm looking for an answer saying, "Ohh, what if this means to keep Him in the center?" or "What if it's our heart without Christ in the center?" Then I stopped and asked God and I heard in my spirit, "It's just a missing piece. Find it." I had to laugh! Throughout this process, I didn't have to ask God one thing. He showed me and it was so much bigger than my thoughts that I knew it could have never been me that came up with it. I saw how quickly we can over-spiritualize things and it blew my mind. We know when He is leading us, yet we still try to help Him. Well, God has shown me very clearly in this season that He does not need my help and I can tell you that He doesn't need yours either.

> **God has the answers and all we need to do is listen.**

God has the answers and all we need to do is listen. When we begin to look for the answers ourselves, we allow confusion to enter which will have us operating and moving in things God never said. This only prolongs our process. This process taught me that I know God's voice. Just the moment of me seeking on my own, brought so much anxiety that I immediately missed God's peace. I was able to stop myself from going on a derailed path by simply asking God.

Before God led me to this process, I would literally allow the spirit of confusion to consume me. The enemy can't create anything, but he surely can manipulate. I would allow insecurities from my past hurt in my marriage to make me literally go backwards. The voices in my head were surely louder than the sweet whisper of God and I would set out to defend myself at all costs. This is what happened when the person from the past tried to reach out to my husband. I allowed myself to believe the lie. The problem is, once we do that the devil comes to water the seeds we allowed to be planted. There was one thing after the other that fed the delusion that I had come to accept as reality. I forgot to seek God, I was reacting from a place of hurt, and all I wanted to do was find a place of comfort. Well, that came in the form of a familiar spirit in a man that was just as broken as I was. As crazy as it sounds, I'm happy it all unfolded the way it did. Otherwise, I could still be stuck in the process of getting over my own ways.

When we go through hardships often, we cleave to what's comfortable. For me, it was talking to other people who seemed to understand me better. For you, it may be alcohol, drugs, sex, cutting, masturbation, fighting, etc. Just remember that whatever your struggle is, God speaks and if we don't take time in silence with God to hear Him we often allow His voice to be overshadowed by the negative thoughts in our minds.

Process 8: Know His Voice

Take a Minute to Pray and Process

Father, today I ask for clarity, peace, and understanding. Help me to know that I hear your voice without a doubt. Lord, help me to remember to call on you before I act on my own understanding. Father, some days are harder than others, but I have declared, and I continue to declare that I will seek you first in all things that I do. Help me to break every stronghold or addiction that is keeping me from growing in the way that you would have me. Today, Father, I put all childish things away. I want and need more of you in order to break free from _____ **(call it out)**. *Father my spirit is willing, my flesh is weak, but I know in my weakness you are my strength. Help me God to not only hear your voice but to be bold enough to follow it no matter where you take me. In Jesus' matchless name, Amen.*

In what ways does God speak to you? *(If you aren't sure ask Him to make you sensitive to His voice.)*

How did reading this lesson make you feel?

What did you take away from this process?

Journal your thoughts on the next page...

Stuck in the Process

Process 9: Trust His Word

I was now a quarter of the way through the puzzle, and I had been working for a few days with no tug in my spirit from the Lord. After the last lesson I dared not to question why. I just did what I knew I should in the time frame that I was allowed to do it. As I was working on it, I found myself out of pieces that could work in the area that I was working on. This time I was not stuck for long. When I first began, I would be stuck for hours sometimes, even days. This time I was reminded of the Transition Piece. Man! That spoke to my heart. Why? Because God reminded me with that, that in our process, whatever it may be, His word will come back to us to lead us, which is why it is important for us to be in His word and store it in our hearts.

> His word will come back to us to lead us, which is why it is important for us to be in His word and store it in our hearts.

Now I know "Transition Piece" is not in the Bible. However, can you imagine in the middle of a storm hearing God remind you of His word? This is what this process taught me that He will remind us of His word. This is why we must seek Him and allow His word to minister to us. Throughout this book God had reminded me of so many scriptures; scriptures that I didn't even think I retained but my longing for His word, my longing to hear sermons, my longing to be in His presence has allowed His word to be imparted to me. The same way Jesus defeated Satan with the word of God is the same way we must. It is our

Stuck in the Process

weapon, and it is the only armor that will work against the enemy of our souls.

On the healing journey that my husband and I have been on for the past year and a half there were times that I would default to, "I just don't want to do this anymore." I had adapted this habit to protect myself from him constantly saying that he would leave. It irritated the spirit of rejection that I had to overcome from childhood. So, one day we had a disagreement over something I saw as small, but he saw as big, and my husband thought that ignoring me for a day or so was the answer. I tried to immediately apologize and make it right, but he wasn't being the easiest to work with. I found myself feeling isolated and the enemy began to use his inability to have healthy conflict resolution as a tool against me.

I had to cast down so many thoughts and I had to stop my old habits from resurfacing. Then I began to apply each process that you have read thus far. I put God in the middle of the disagreement and vented to Him about my husband's behavior. I also constantly sought Him for my error, instead of just pointing the finger at my husband. I made sure I stayed in the face of God because this time I realized that I won't look back at what I used to do, despite what my husband does or does not do. In my pressing God gave me peace and most importantly He reminded me of His word. The difference between now and then was this time when I heard His Word, I trusted it. I didn't dismiss it or keep looking for an answer that would validate me. I took the answer that corrected me and challenged me to see things from my husband's perspective. I learned that if it's big to him then it needs to be bigger to me. This posture eliminates a person feeling overlooked and unheard in a marriage. God used my hurtful experiences of feeling unheard as the catalyst for me to empathize with my husband. In a marriage we should capitalize on each other's strengths. Seeing how I knew a better way to resolve conflict I was challenged with the task to lovingly teach my husband what God had shown me. Please know that our spouses are not our competition. I could not let it go into a battle of who was right or wrong, but I had to acknowledge the battle that we both fight together spiritually on a daily basis.

Take a Minute to Pray and Process

Father, when I feel weak help me to trust your Word. When my faith is low, help me to remember that you aren't a man that you should lie. Today I declare that your Word is sufficient. Help me to remember that in every situation I have the ability to look beyond my feelings. Today, God, I ask that you give me peace even in the midst of this process. I believe that my walls are falling, and I pray that I continue to have a mind made up to trust you in my vulnerability. In every situation that I may be stuck in, let me reach the breaking point that will allow me to apply every process in this book to my life. Help me to see you in the midst of my circumstances and remind me, Father, that I am not doing this alone. In Jesus' name, Amen!

Do you trust God?

How did reading this lesson make you feel?

What did you take away from this process?

Journal your thoughts on the next page...

Phase 3:
The Chrysalis/ Consecration

For the caterpillar to become a butterfly it must have a time of isolation in the form of a Chrysalis[13]. This is where the butterfly begins to take form into a new creation. As we walk with Christ, we begin to change. We are considered a new creation in Christ and old things have passed away; all things have become new" according to (2 Corinthians 5:17)[14]. However, consecration is where we are prepared to begin to walk in our authority as Daughters and Sons of God. We are now in a place to be equipped to be disciples in the way that God intended. We begin to realize that who we hang around, what we listen to, and where we go matters. We begin to change not because we think we are better than others, but because we love God and want to honor Him in all that we do. In this phase we have learned to continue to choose His way, that we must know His voice, and that we need to trust His word.

Process 10: Remember His Promise

"Let your conduct be without covetousness; be content with such things as you have. For He Himself has said, 'I will never leave you nor forsake you.'" (Hebrews 13:5-6)[15]

One of the things I did not discuss throughout the process of my puzzle experience was that my children would continue to come and work on the puzzle little by little. I wanted to tell them to not touch it at one point, afraid that they may lose a piece. However, I was led not to tell them that, so even if it was just a piece here and there, they helped. I didn't speak of this part before because I did not know that God was even using them in this process.

At this point I was about a month and a half into working, sticking to the days and times that I was allotted to do so. I had a very small corner left and was very close to being done. This day seemed different though. Somehow, I knew that when I got up to leave the table that I would not return to the puzzle in the way that I left it.

I went on about my day. The weekends were not days that I was allowed to work on the puzzle to prioritize family time and other responsibilities, so I had learned to detach and focus on other things. It was Sunday evening, and I was preparing for bed. My oldest son entered our room and said, "Mom, come here! I have to show you something important." I said, "Can it wait until tomorrow?" He replied, "No not really." I continued to prepare myself and as I did so, I heard in my spirit clear as day, "It is finished." I knew without a doubt in my mind that he had completed my puzzle. A part of me wanted to be upset because I wanted to finish this beautiful journey that God had me start but that was my flesh. My spirit was joyful that my son had watched this journey and felt led to assist. I told him that I would be right out. Once I was decent, I entered the part of my bedroom where my husband was laying on the bed and I said, "I know what it is." He said, "How do you know?" I told him what I heard in my spirit, and his mouth dropped.

I made my way downstairs with my husband right behind me, and all four of our children were surrounding the table that had my now almost-completed puzzle. I looked at my son and he handed me the last piece and said, "I felt led to let you have this honor." I was reminded of a scripture that God would finish the work that he started in you. (Philippians 1:6)

This lesson was simple. It was God's way of showing me the role of the Holy Spirit. The Bible says that He is our help and often times in our lives we are looking for Him to move in the way that we want. The thing is, He always moves in the way that is most helpful to us even if we don't want it. My children went on this journey with me. I got to see how what I go through truly impacts everyone in our home. They saw my frustration, my posture change, the reaction to the lessons I learned. They went through the process with me daily and wanted to help me get through.

They learned patience that they didn't have before; they learned how to have quiet time with God. In return I learned that the childish ways from the little girl buried

Process 10: Remember His Promise

inside of me all of those years, just like this puzzle experience, would have impacted them too, but in a negative way. Had I continued to react before thinking, being "feeling" led, or moving into "flight" every time things went bad, they would have watched that process too. They would have lost the one thing I wanted most for them all due to my inability to forgive, grow, and truly let God move in my life. This process was life changing for me; I finally got to see the enemy that was within me.

Abba Father, thank you for not leaving me where I was. I thank you for loving me beyond my hurt. You used the person who I felt broke me to restore me, and I will forever be grateful to you for that. I love you for knowing how to reach me. The journey of this puzzle was different, but I can honestly say that you, God, used a puzzle to change my life. I am forever grateful and humbled that you saved a wretch like me.

Take a Minute to Pray and Process

Father, help me to see your promises unfold in my life. Forgive me for my unbelief but today I ask that you restore my hope in the promise. Let me have a child like faith, that the work you started in me, you will complete. I surrender to your will for my life, and I will no longer try to take the pen away from you as you rewrite my story. In Jesus' name, Amen.

What biblical promises do you declare over your life?

Do you invite the Holy Spirit in to help you?

How did reading this lesson make you feel?

What did you take away from this process?

Journal your thoughts on the next page...

Stuck in the Process

My Prayer For You!

My prayer for you is that God will allow you to identify where you may be stuck. That God heals your heart and that you remember no matter where you are in your process that you are a Son or Daughter of the Most High King before anything else. I pray that you apply each step that God led me through to your own situation. That you realize that step by step and day by day God will change your whole countenance. I pray that every wall you've built is broken down so that He may begin to move in you. I pray that every process that God has led me to write penetrates your heart. I pray, Father, that they receive from you the way that I did, openly and eagerly. Give them their own experience God so that they may begin to apply what you have led me to write in this book to their own process.

Phase 4:
The Butterfly/ Disciple

A butterfly's number one job is a pollinator. When they feed on the nectar of a flower, they encounter pollen. The material of the pollen attaches to the butterfly and is deposited in other flowers that they visit[16]. After our time of consecration, we are commanded to as the word says in (Matthew 28: 19-20)[17] *"Go therefore and make disciples of all the nations, baptizing them in the name of the Father and of the Son and of the Holy Spirit, teaching them to observe all things that I have commanded you; and lo, I am with you always, even to the end of the age."*

> **For some we will present Christ but for others we will need to re-present Christ in the way that He intended.**

As disciples we are to go and spread the good news! Just as this butterfly leaves a deposit into every other flower it touches, we also should when we meet people. We are the representation of Christ and for some we will present Christ but for others we will need to re-present Christ in the way that He intended.

Embracing the Process

Now that you know how to embrace a process, you can begin walking in the fullness of who God has called you to be. Just remember His promise. I do want you to know that everyone's process looks different. My issue to process and grow from was my marriage but yours could be a broken relationship with your parents, or children, etc. The steps learned in the process are all that matters. God used a puzzle to teach me these steps because he knows how to reach me and now, I share them with you believing that God will let them help you as well. When I asked God why a puzzle, he reminded me of my earliest memories with one. He needed me to go back to a childlike state, and then he showed me it was used because I couldn't rush the process.

> Now that you know how to embrace a process, you can begin walking in the fullness of who God has called you to be.

Please be patient with yourself as you grow. God showed me the Life Cycle of a Butterfly because they too are uniquely sculpted and individually designed like us. Our journeys are not a one-size-fits-all kind of thing. So, remember what the late Theodore Roosevelt said, "Comparison is the thief of joy."[18] There are no butterflies that are identical, and neither are our processes of healing and growing into the person God has created us to be. Some of us will struggle kind of like I did for years. However, some others will quickly embrace the changes and begin to "fly."

Just one more thing...

After all the phases you have seen of a butterfly's life cycle the one thing that I must tell you is that even once the butterfly emerges from the chrysalis, it cannot immediately fly[19]. So don't rush the healing, the changes, or the renewed heart that God has done in you. Don't feel the need to rush into any title or position either. Each step matters, so be patient with yourself and allow as much time as needed. Just remember, if you are embracing the process, then you are no longer stuck.

Congratulations!

Embracing the Process

Process Completed

End Notes

1. The Bible. The New Living Translation Version. YouVersion, app version 9.15, Life. Church, 2023.
2. The Bible. The King James Version. YouVersion, app version 9.15, Life. Church, 2023.
3. The Bible. The New King James Version. YouVersion, app version 9.15, Life. Church, 2023.
4. "Life Cycle of a Butterfly." Smatclass4kids.Com, 1 Jan. 2023, smartclass4kids.com/life-cycle-of-a-butterfly/. Accessed 27 Jul. 2023.
5. The Bible. The New King James Version. YouVersion, app version 9.15, Life. Church, 2023.
6. The Bible. The New King James Version. YouVersion, app version 9.15, Life. Church, 2023.
7. The Bible. The King James Version. YouVersion, app version 9.15, Life. Church, 2023.
8. The Bible. The New King James Version. YouVersion, app version 9.15, Life. Church, 2023.
9. The Bible. The New King James Version. YouVersion, app version 9.15, Life. Church, 2023.
10. "Life Cycle of a Butterfly." Smatclass4kids.Com, 1 Jan. 2023, smartclass4kids.com/life-cycle-of-a-butterfly/. Accessed 27 Jul. 2023.
11. The Bible. The New King James Version. YouVersion, app version 9.15, Life. Church, 2023.
12. The Bible. The New King James Version. YouVersion, app version 9.15, Life. Church, 2023.
13. "Life Cycle of a Butterfly." Smatclass4kids.Com, 1 Jan. 2023, smartclass4kids.com/life-cycle-of-a-butterfly/. Accessed 27 Jul. 2023.
14. The Bible. The New King James Version. YouVersion, app version 9.15, Life. Church, 2023.
15. The Bible. The New King James Version. YouVersion, app version 9.15, Life. Church, 2023.
16. "Life Cycle of a Butterfly." Smatclass4kids.Com, 1 Jan. 2023, smartclass4kids.com/life-cycle-of-a-butterfly/. Accessed 27 Jul. 2023.
17. The Bible. The New King James Version. YouVersion, app version 9.15, Life. Church, 2023.
18. "Brainy Quotes." Theodore Roosevelt Quotes, 3 Oct. 2001, www.brainyquote.com/authors/theodore-roosevelt-quotes. Accessed 27 Jul. 2023.
19. "Life Cycle of a Butterfly." Smatclass4kids.Com, 1 Jan. 2023, smartclass4kids.com/life-cycle-of-a-butterfly/. Accessed 27 Jul. 2023.

www.ingramcontent.com/pod-product-compliance
Lightning Source LLC
Chambersburg PA
CBHW071143060526
44107CB00131B/192